Mission

LIVING FOR THE PURPOSES OF GOD

Scott Nelson

Foreword by Alan Hirsch

InterVarsity Press
P.O. Box 1400, Downers Grove, IL 60515-1426
World Wide Web: www.ivpress.com
E-mail: email@ivpress.com

InterVarsity Press® is the book-publishing division of InterVarsity Christian Fellowship/USA®, a movement of students and faculty active on campus at hundreds of universities, colleges and schools of nursing in the United States of America, and a member movement of the International Fellowship of Evangelical Students. For information about local and regional activities, write Public Relations Dept., InterVarsity Christian Fellowship/USA, 6400 Schroeder Rd., P.O. Box 7895, Madison, WI 53707-7895, or visit the IVCF website at <www.intervarsity.org>.

While all stories in this book are true, some names and identifying information in this book have been changed to protect the privacy of the individuals involved.

Cover design: Cindy Kiple
Interior design: Beth Hagenberg

ISBN 978-0-8308-1044-4 (print)
ISBN 978-0-8308-9572-4 (digital)

Printed in the United States of America ∞

InterVarsity Press is committed to protecting the environment and to the responsible use of natural resources. As a member of Green Press Initiative we use recycled paper whenever possible. To learn more about the Green Press Initiative, visit <www.greenpressinitiative.org>.

Library of Congress Cataloging-in Publication Data
A catalog record for this book is available from the Library of Congress.

P 20 19 18 17 16 15 14 13 12 11 10 9 8 7 6 5 4 3 2 1
Y 30 29 28 27 26 25 24 23 22 21 20 19 18 17 16 15 14 13

CONTENTS

FOREWORD

For the better part of two decades now, *missional* has been equal parts buzzword and byword in the contemporary church.

Many church leaders have decried the trendiness of the term, predicting that it will eventually go the way of all fads, and that responsible church leadership involves simply waiting it out, keeping the faith. And it's hard to deny the trendiness of the term: as the editors of *Leadership Journal* noted in their preface to an article of mine five years ago, "A quick search on Google uncovers the presence of 'missional communities,' 'missional leaders,' 'missional worship,' even 'missional seating,' and 'missional coffee.'"[1] The closer the application of the term approaches absurdity, the less seriously we are inclined to take it.

And yet over the same period the concept of a missional church has proved its durability. Conference after conference has organized itself around the concept that God is on mission in the world, and that as means to the end of achieving his mission God has created a church. Seminary after seminary has reconfigured its core curricula to take the model of a church on mission seriously, and to train pastors and other leaders to understand themselves as missionaries first, "keepers" of the faith a distant second. What so many have dismissed as a fad or a trend, substantial and growing numbers of people are recognizing as a paradigm shift.

Of course, any number of paradigm-shifting conversations are taking place at the conceptual level among the leadership of the global church at any given moment. Many such conversations bubble up only to dissipate; such in-house deliberation is part of the long history of the faith. It is in this historical reality that the durability and trajectory of the missional church conversation reveals its significance. More than a mere theoretical conversation, the missional church bears the marks of a true movement—broad-based, but with a cohesive sense of self-understanding; goal-driven, but deeply rooted in principles and conviction; critical of the status quo, yet always motivated by the greater good. Christianity itself has always been a movement, inspired by the God who created the world and called it good, who so loved the world that he gave his only Son for it.

Any movement over time has the capacity to atrophy, to be distracted by its own sense of self-preservation, to be enthralled by the beauty of its past accomplishments and the currency of its cultural power. But the original vision of the movement relentlessly beckons, confronting our self-congratulation and propelling us toward the greater good of our original calling.

At Forge we have always said that the best critique of the bad is the practice of the better. With this series of guides on missional practices we are trying to help create a more productive and better future for a church now in systemic decline. We believe the church was made for far more than mere self-preservation, and certainly not for retreat. We were made to be a highly transformative Jesus movement; we had best get on with being that. To do this we need to redisciple the church into its calling and mission. Discipleship is a huge key, and for this we need tools.

Every movement requires the education—the *formation*—of its people. I believe the next phase of the movement that is the missional church resides not so much in seminaries or elder meetings as around the tables of people of faith wherever they find themselves. These Forge Guides for Missional Conversation are intended to facilitate those conversations—to help you, wherever you are, to step together into the flow of God's mission in the world.

Scott Nelson is particularly equipped to facilitate such conversations. He has held leadership positions in traditional churches and studied the church's mission while pursuing his doctorate. He has taken on the responsibility of the theological direction of Forge Mission Training Network in America even as he has developed a missional community in the neighborhood where he lives. The mission of God is thoroughly integrated into Scott's life—heart and soul, mind and strength—which is as it is intended to be.

Each of the five guides that make up this series will be valuable on its own; thoroughly scriptural, accessibly theological, highly practical and fundamentally spiritual, each will give you a fuller appreciation of what it means to be a follower of Jesus on God's mission. Taken together, however, they are a sort of curriculum for a movement: you and your friends will be fully equipped for every good work that God has in mind for you in the place where you find yourself.

Our missionary God created a church in service to his mission. We were made for a movement. Read on if you're ready to move!

Alan Hirsch

INTRODUCTION TO THE FORGE GUIDES

I've been obsessed with the idea of helping Christians develop a missionary imagination for their daily lives ever since I began to develop such an imagination back in 2007. My missionary imagination began at a church staff retreat. I was asked what I thought our church staff should do if God dropped us all from a helicopter into our city with absolutely no resources and asked us to start a church. While thinking of my answer to this question, I realized I would have to take on the mindset of a missionary—go out to the people, learn who they are, get involved in their lives, care about what they care about. The years that have passed since that fateful question have been an amazing journey for me. I quit my job, dove into full-time study of the missionary mindset in Christian congregations, began exploring ways to live like a missionary in the condominium complex where my wife and I currently live, and teamed up with the Forge America Mission Training Network to be a part of an organization that actively seeks to implant a missionary mindset in Christians and their faith communities.

I've written these guides to help you ask some of the same questions that I asked, and to help you think about what it might look like if you, your group or your church were to develop a missionary imagination for everyday living. There are at least three reasons why it is crucially important that you ask these questions and develop a missionary imagination.

The first reason is the cultural changes that are taking place in Western contexts. Changes such as increasing globalization, religious and cultural pluralism, huge advances in science and technology, the collapse of many modern principles and the growth of postmodernism, and the secularization of the West have drastically altered many cultural landscapes. If the gospel is to be proclaimed faithfully and effectively in these changing contexts, Christians must be missionaries who study cultures in order to translate the gospel so that all can clearly hear it. Simply saying and doing the same things in the same ways as generations past is no longer effective.

A second reason it is vitally important for Christians to develop a missionary mindset is the crisis facing the institutional church. The many different statistical studies that measure the size and influence of the church in the United States are sobering. Despite the explosion of megachurches, congregations in the United States as a whole consist of older people and fewer participants, and experience decreased influence in local contexts. The institutional, established church is experiencing a serious internal crisis as contexts change and congregations fail to adapt. Christians must regain a sense of their missionary calling if the trend of a diminishing role for the Christian faith is to be reversed in the West.

Third, I see evidence of a common longing for a deeper, lived-out faith among many Christians, especially among emerging generations. I've felt it and so have many others who I have read and talked with. It is the feeling that something about the way I am participating in church and faith seems to be missing; it seems to be too easy or too shallow. Conversations with Christians across the country reveal a longing to be challenged, to do something significant with their faith, to make a difference in the lives of people both globally and locally. By developing a missionary imagination for everyday living, these Christians develop a mindset that can lead to deeper expressions of faith, which ultimately reorient a person's whole life around what God is doing and wants to do in this world.

My life story and the three reasons I just listed compelled me to write and use these conversation guides for my own small group. Perhaps you have had a similar experience, or maybe one of the three reasons prompted you to pick up the guides. Even if not, I sincerely hope the questions contained in these guides will infect your minds, as they did mine. And I sincerely hope the mission of God will infect your lives, as I pray every day for it to infect mine.

USING THE FORGE GUIDES

My focus in creating these guides has not been to give you all the answers. I firmly believe you and the members of your group need to discern the answers for yourselves, and further, to generate the creativity that will shape your imagination for what a missionary lifestyle might look like in your life and community. My task in creating these guides is to help you ask good questions.

While creating these guides, I kept coming back to the idea of minimalist running shoes. The science behind these increasingly popular shoes claims that the human body is naturally equipped to run. Big, cushiony, fancy running shoes are not only unnecessary but counterproductive. What runners really need is a simple shoe that accentuates their natural abilities, encourages proper running form and protects their feet from environmental hazards.

These guides are designed to be a lot like minimalist running shoes. They offer the bare minimum you will need to ask good questions, seek innovative answers and develop a new imagination. The guides do not do the work for you. Rather, let them draw out your natural ability to hear from Scripture, to think about the world around you, to wonder about who God is and to imagine ways you can live as a missionary.

These four practices appear in each lesson under the headings

"Dwelling in the Word," "Contextual Analysis," "Theological Reflection" and "Missionary Imagination." I have identified relevant biblical texts, but it is your job to listen for how God is speaking to you and your group. The guides also provide probing questions about your local context, but it is your job to do the analysis required to provide the answers. Similarly, the guides will provide theological content and point to basic principles of missional living, but it is your job to reflect on the nature of God and how he is asking you to live out his mission in your context.

To help you understand what you will be doing as you work through the conversation guides, a brief description of each basic practice follows. Please note that some groups will naturally gravitate to some of the practices more than to others. Don't feel the need to go through each section with a fine-toothed comb. There is more material than will likely be needed for most group gatherings, so be flexible with the practices and allow the group to choose how much time to allocate to each section.

Practice 1: Dwelling in the Word

Each group gathering begins with a time to hear from Scripture through communal reading and listening.[2] Dwelling in the same text over a period of six weeks (or more!) will allow your group to begin developing a shared imagination and a shared openness to the many things God may want to say and do through the text.

The group listens to the passage, reflects in silence for a few moments and then breaks into pairs to discuss two questions about the text. After sufficient time has passed (while allowing adequate time for the remainder of the session), the group gathers together. Individuals share what their partners heard in the text while answers are recorded. This section concludes with the group asking, What might God be up to in this passage for us today?

Sometimes people will doubt the value of returning to the same text time after time, but trust the process and believe that the Bible is the living Word of God. The more you continue to return to the same text, the more you will find blessing at the insight you gain, the habits you learn, the imagination you develop and the community you form.

One final point can help you get started on the right foot: dwelling in the Word is about hearing from God's Word and hearing from each other. Each person is responsible for helping one other person give voice to what she or he heard from the text and to then be an advocate for that person's thoughts in the larger group. These practices are intended to help the group create an environment where thoughts are safely shared and members listen deeply to one another. Over time, dwelling in the Word is a powerful tool that can form a community of the Spirit where the presence and power of the Spirit is both welcome and expected.

Practice 2: Contextual Analysis

Missionaries know that the gospel must be translated—literally and figuratively—into local contexts. Every local culture is unique and will hear and receive the gospel in different ways. A good missionary learns to understand local cultures so that he or she can inculturate the gospel in a way specifically tailored to a specific people group. At times of inculturation into new contexts, the gospel has proven to be the most effective at bringing about radical transformation in individuals, communities and whole societies. The Forge Guides for Missional Conversation are designed to help Christian communities inculturate and translate the gospel into their local contexts by facilitating shared practices of contextual analysis during group gatherings.

Practices of contextual analysis will focus on three main areas: describing the local context, discerning what God is already doing in the local context and wondering together what God might want to do in the local context. A variety of ways to practice contextual analysis are provided in each session. Sometimes the group will simply have questions to answer. At other times they will be asked to complete an activity or reflect personally. It is hoped that the variety of practices provided will lead the group to a new understanding of their context and will help the group faithfully proclaim and live out the gospel in new and exciting ways that transform the members of the group and the world around them.

Practice 3: Theological Reflection

David Kelsey defines theology as the search to understand and know God truly.[3] Theology in this sense becomes wisdom in relationship to God. Much like understanding an instruction manual about building a bike leads to the ability to build that bike, searching to understand God brings about some ability to relate with God through spiritual practices, worship and faith. Those who know God can sense and participate in what God is doing in the world around them.

The section on theological reflection is designed to help your group seek to know God truly so that the group might become wise in relationship to God. It will encourage you to actively wonder about who God is and what he is up to in the world. Scripture passages and a few reflection questions will be provided for the group to study. Sometimes other sources of theological reflection—such as distinct church traditions, church history or other texts—will be provided. No matter what specific content is provided for you to reflect on, the goal will always be the same and that is for your group to ask, What can we know about who God is and what God does? How does this influence the way we relate to God and join with him in what he is doing?

Practice 4: Missionary Imagination

Each session will conclude with a time for developing a missionary imagination through conversation, personal reflection, group affirmation, prayer or a variety of other activities. The time set aside for missionary imagination is intended to help each individual in the group gain a better sense of his or her own missionary calling, and also to help the group as a whole develop a missionary imagination for its existence. I've tried particularly hard to provide a wide variety of activities in this section. The goal of these activities as well as their very nature is meant to help you and your group break the mold when it comes to calling, vision and imagination. When my own small group went through this material, we had a blast doing things like drawing pictures, sharing stories, writing limericks and making collages, as well as answering the more conventional discussion questions. Have fun with this section and do your best to encourage one another to be imaginative, innovative and experimental in missionary living.

Before We Meet Again

Midweek assignments are given at the end of each week's session. These assignments are fun little projects designed to help group members continue to think about the session throughout the week. For instance, one assignment might ask members to take pictures of three things during the week that they think represent the work of God in the world. Time for the group to review the midweek assignment is often built into the next week's session. I strongly encourage your group to complete these assignments whenever possible. My own group really enjoyed them!

Recording and Reflecting

As your group talks through these guides, my final recommendation is to take notes during the discussions, whether individually or through a general secretary. These records will help you discern patterns and commonalities that may help you see what God is doing in your lives.

INTRODUCTION

Mission: Living for the Purposes of God

If I could give someone just one book to read about the missional church it would most certainly be *Transforming Mission* by the late David Bosch.[4] *Transforming Mission* is widely recognized as one of the foundational works in the missional church movement and has played a significant role in establishing the historical roots of the movement (see "A Brief Introduction to the Theology and History of the Missional Church Conversation" at ivpress.com). It is a great read for anyone interested in the mission of God and the mission of the church.

In the book Bosch makes a couple of powerful claims that help introduce the direction of the conversation guide your group is about to use. Bosch suggests that Christian faith and Christian existence are intrinsically *missionary in nature*. Being missionary by nature means the church is involved in activity locally and globally that is transformative in every context and culture. Mission happens when the whole church brings the whole gospel to the whole world. It is a lifestyle that announces to the world that "God is a God-for-people."[5]

Put another way, to live as a Christian is to live on mission with God. This conversation guide is the first of five in a series focused on developing a missionary imagination for everyday living. The focus of this guide is to help you and your group begin to imagine what a life that is *missionary by nature* might look like. The guide will help you determine what a life defined by God's purposes in your local context entails. Essentially, the guide will lead you to think about God's nature, God's purposes, what these look like in your context and how they shape the way you live.

Session One

LIVING AS CHRIST'S AMBASSADORS

Missionaries have a lot in common with ambassadors. A missionary is a person sent to promote a particular belief among a foreign group or country, while an ambassador acts as a representative of either a country or an idea to another country or group of people. In both cases there is a particular lifestyle appropriate to the role, which requires making the ideas or norms of one thing understandable to another. For our purposes think of the lifestyle that has the distinctive nature or qualities of one sent to live as God's ambassador as "mission-shaped living." The goal of today's conversation is to begin to discover mission-shaped living—what it looks like to let God's mission and purposes shape our daily lives. Begin the conversation by turning to 2 Corinthians 5:11–6:1.

Dwelling in the Word

- Begin in prayer, inviting the Spirit to guide your group as you dwell in the text.

- Read aloud 2 Corinthians 5:11–6:1.
- Allow a few moments of silence after the reading has been completed to reflect on the passage and what stands out to you.
- Break into pairs (preferably with someone you don't know well) and discuss the following questions. Use this time to practice listening to each other as well as to the text.
    - What in the text captured your imagination?
    - What question would you most like to ask a biblical scholar?
- Gather once again as a large group and share your partners' responses.
- Review these responses and discuss: What might God be up to in the passage for us today?

Contextual Analysis

An ambassador is sent into a certain crosscultural context to represent the interests of the sending party. Ambassadors also serve as mediators between those who sent them and those who host them in their new surroundings.

1. How would you describe your group's context? Be as specific as you can.

2. What words do you think describe your context? Given this list, what name would you give to your context?

3. God gives his ambassadors the ministry of reconciliation, asking them to share his message with others so they too might be reconciled to God. What would it look like if your local context were reconciled to God? What would change? Remain the same?

- Break into small groups of 3-4. On a separate piece of paper draw a before-and-after picture of your local context as it now is (before) and what it would look like if it were reconciled to God (after). Describe your picture to the group once all groups are finished. Keep the drawing some place prominent for the next six weeks.

Theological Reflection: *The God Who Sends His People*

The Gospel of Luke teaches about God as a sending God. Reflecting on key passages from Luke reveals much to us about who God is, what he is doing and who he chooses to carry out his purposes.

- Break into pairs. Read Jesus' description of himself as sent by God in Luke 4:16-21, and Jesus' sending of his followers in both Luke 9:1-6 and Luke 10:1-20. Reflect on the following after reading each text.

4. Reflect on the God who sends. What do you learn about who he is, what he wants, what he is doing and so forth?

5. Reflect on the people who God sends. What can you learn about them?

6. Reflect on what God sends people to be, speak and do. What do these things reveal about God, his mission and his people?

Missionary Imagination

7. Identify and list the questions you think you would need to ask and answer in order to understand how to live as ambassadors for God in your local context.

8. As a group, come up with some preliminary answers to the questions you identified.

9. In what ways is your group currently living as coworkers with God and ambassadors for his mission?

10. How might your group need to adapt to be more effective coworkers and ambassadors?

Before We Meet Again

- Continue to read and reflect on 2 Corinthians 5:11–6:1 and the passages from Luke. Record your thoughts here:

- Take three pictures or three sets of pictures and bring them to share with the group. These pictures should represent three things: ways or places you see God at work in your local context, places where your local context is in need of reconciliation to God, examples of people or institutions who are serving as God's ambassadors. Describe the pictures you took and your reason for taking them.
- Write one sentence that describes the purposes of God as you currently understand them. Record it in the following space.

Session Two

LIVING IN RIGHTEOUSNESS, NOT JUST RELIGIOUSNESS

A friend of mine once complained to me that he had spent thirteen of his last fifteen evenings at his church building rehearsing for an upcoming play, attending special programs, and practicing with the worship team for Sunday services and for a special holiday service. My friend remarked that he felt he barely had time for anything but church. He then asked me what I had been up to, and I said I had probably spent thirteen of my last fifteen evenings trying to live like a missionary among my neighbors by hanging out with a neighbor whose father had just died, doing minor projects and repairs for two different single women who live near me, and having some of our neighbors over for dinner.

The profound difference in how we had spent our time struck us both, and I think we realized that sometimes our religiousness leads us to righteousness, but at other times it keeps us from doing the good we ought to do. It is often tempting to think living for God's purposes can be equated to being religious. The goal of today's conversation, however, is to explore God's demands that his people be righteous and not just religious. Keep this goal in mind as you begin.

Take a few moments to share your assignments and reflections since the last meeting.

Dwelling in the Word

- Begin in prayer, inviting the Spirit to guide your group as you dwell in the text.
- Read aloud 2 Corinthians 5:11–6:1.
- Allow a few moments of silence after the reading has been completed to reflect on the passage and what stands out to you.
- Break into pairs (preferably with someone you don't know well) and discuss the following questions. Use this time to practice listening to each other as well as to the text.
    - What in the text captured your imagination?
    - What question would you most like to ask a biblical scholar?
- Gather once again as a large group and share your partners' responses.
- Review these responses and discuss: What might God be up to in the passage for us today?

Contextual Analysis

Righteousness is a lifestyle. It consists of attitudes, actions and beliefs as a person lives rightly toward God, others and self. Let's begin by thinking about living rightly toward others.

1. As you did during session 1, begin by considering the context God has sent your group to. How, if at all, has your thinking changed from session 1?

2. Reflect on the lifestyle(s) of people in your context (including those in your group). What do those in your context seem to value most?

3. What adjective(s) could best sum up the lifestyle(s) within your context? What do you notice about these adjectives? Are they harsh? Lenient?

4. What adjectives do you think might describe a righteous lifestyle in this context? How are they similar to the adjectives listed above? How are they different?

Theological Reflection: *The God Who Desires More Than Ritual*

Those who wish to live rightly toward God often develop habits and rituals to help sustain a right lifestyle. It is a normal and necessary part of trying to orient all of one's life toward God in a right way. Early on in history God himself gave his people quite a few habits, rituals and practices to follow, and commanded them to closely keep these (consider Exodus, Leviticus, Numbers and Deuteronomy). Scripture makes it clear, however, that God has always desired more than rituals and religiousness. God desires his people to live in righteousness, and often sent his prophets (including Jesus) to convey that message to them.

- Break into pairs and read some or all of the following texts: Isaiah 1; Isaiah 58; Zechariah 7; Matthew 23; James 1:19-27.

5. For each text record the religious practices and describe the righteous lifestyle that God desired more so than the practices.

6. Review both lists. What generalizations can you make about what God condemns and what God desires?

7. Based on these texts, what do you learn about God? What do you learn about God's mission and God's purposes?

8. Consider the one-sentence description of God's purposes that you wrote during the week. Share it with the group (if you want). How has today's theological reflection modified your sentence?

Missionary Imagination

Righteousness toward God should always lead to right living toward or with others. As the study today has tried to show, it often has been easier for God's people to develop practices for living rightly toward him than for living rightly toward others.

9. What practices have you or your group developed to live rightly toward God?

10. Have these practices led to right living toward others? If yes, how? If no, why not?

11. What practices have you or your group already developed to live rightly toward others?

12. Based on today's conversation, what practices could you develop to live more rightly toward God and others?

Before We Meet Again

- Continue to read and reflect on 2 Corinthians 5:11–6:1 and one of the texts from today's conversation. Record your thoughts here:

- Modify your one-sentence description of God's purposes (if necessary). Add to it a one-sentence description of how to live for God's purposes. Write (or rewrite) both.

- Think about your religious practices and your lifestyle. If God were to speak to you through a prophet, what might he say? Write yourself a message from God similar in form and tone to the prophetic texts you read during this session.

- Grab a local newspaper and spend 5-10 minutes scanning through different articles. Record your observations about your context's hopes, fears and goals.

Session Three

LIVING IN LIGHT OF THE NEW BEGINNING

See, I will create
new heavens and a new earth.
The former things will not be remembered,
nor will they come to mind.
But be glad and rejoice forever
in what I will create,
for I will create Jerusalem to be a delight
and its people a joy.
I will rejoice over Jerusalem
and take delight in my people;
the sound of weeping and of crying
will be heard in it no more.

Isaiah 65:17-19

Any conversation about living for God's purposes must eventually turn to the promises God has given to his people, how these promises reveal God's purposes and how the promises help God's people live for his purposes. Today's conversation builds on the themes of living as God's ambassadors and living in righteousness by exploring what it looks like to live in light of the new beginnings God will ultimately bring for all of his creation.

Take a few moments to share your assignments and reflections since the last meeting, except for the reflections from the newspaper (which will come later).

Dwelling in the Word

- Begin in prayer, inviting the Spirit to guide your group as you dwell in the text.
- Read aloud 2 Corinthians 5:11–6:1.
- Allow a few moments of silence after the reading has been completed to reflect on the passage and what stands out to you.
- Break into pairs (preferably with someone you don't know well) and discuss the following questions. Use this time to practice listening to each other as well as to the text.
    - What in the text captured your imagination?
    - What question would you most like to ask a biblical scholar?
- Gather once again as a large group and share your partners' responses.
- Review these responses and discuss: What might God be up to in the passage for us today?

Contextual Analysis

1. What do people in your context seem to believe about the future?

What are their hopes? What are their fears?

2. What is the ultimate goal or life purpose for people in your context?

3. Share your midweek observations from a newspaper or magazine. What did you notice about your context's hopes, fears and goals?

Theological Reflection: *The God Who Makes All Things New*

Christian living is uniquely shaped by hope. Jürgen Moltmann, a twentieth-century theologian, introduced his now famous work *Theology of Hope* with a beautiful meditation about the power of hope:

> Expectation makes life good, for in expectation man can accept his whole present and find joy not only in its joy but also in its sorrow, happiness not only in its happiness but also in its pain. Thus hope goes on its way through the midst of happiness and pain, because in the promises of God it can see a future also for the transient, the dying and the dead. That is why it can be said that living without hope is like no longer living. Hell is hopelessness, and it is not for nothing that at the entrance to Dante's hell there stand the words: "Abandon hope, all ye who enter here."[6]

4. Restate Moltmann's quote in your own words. Is hope as powerful as he seems to think? Why or why not?

5. Without referencing a Bible, list as many of the following as you can: (1) stories where God makes promises to his people, (2) instances of promises being fulfilled in Scripture and (3) promises that have been made to us or are still outstanding for us today.

6. A key promise God makes to his people is that he will make all things new. Break into pairs and read descriptions of this promise in the following texts: Isaiah 65:17-25; 2 Peter 3:1-15; Revelation 19–22. What do God's promises tell you about his nature? About his purposes? About living for his purposes?

7. Share with the group your one-sentence descriptions of God's purposes and living for God's purposes from your "Before We Meet Again" assignments. Based on the descriptions the group has developed and today's conversation, what have you learned or noticed about God?

Missionary Imagination

The following pattern is clear in Scripture: faith leads to hope, and hope leads to love. God's people place their faith in God because of what they have seen God do in the past. Faith in God leads to hope that God will fulfill his promises for the future as he has done in the past. Hope in God's promises for the future frees God's people to worship God and to serve him by loving others in the present, no matter the circumstances.

8. Break into pairs and read the following biblical passages: Psalm 33; Luke 12:32-47; Romans 4:18–5:5; 1 Thessalonians 4:13–5:11. How do these texts support the pattern of faith leading to hope and hope leading to love?

9. What would it look like for your group to live a life of hope in light of the coming end and new beginning God is bringing?

10. If you truly lived a life of hope, what would change from how you live now? What would remain the same?

Before We Meet Again

- Continue to reflect upon 2 Corinthians 5:11–6:1 and Revelation 19–22. Record your thoughts here:

- Refine (if necessary) your previous one-sentence descriptions of God's purpose and living for God's purpose. Add a third sentence on how God's promises help his people to live for his purposes. Write all three sentences.

- Remind yourself every day that there is a bright and certain future that is awaiting God's people. Record some notes here on how this thought influences your daily life.

- Find something in your context that makes you think of the promised future God is bringing. Be creative! Bring the item you find to the next group meeting and be prepared to describe how it reminds you of the promised future.

Session Four

LIVING TO PROCLAIM GOD'S GOOD NEWS

How beautiful on the mountains
are the feet of those who bring good news,
who proclaim peace,
who bring good tidings,
who proclaim salvation,
who say to Zion,
"Your God reigns!"

Isaiah 52:7

Neither revolution nor reformation can ultimately change a society, rather you must tell a new powerful tale, one so persuasive that it sweeps away the old myths and becomes the preferred story, one so inclusive that it gathers all the bits of our past and our present into a coherent whole, one that even shines some light into the future so that we can take the next step. . . . If you want to change a society, then you have to tell an alternative story.

Ivan Illich

The missional church lives for the purposes of God by proclaiming the good news of God's reign through Jesus Christ. The church continues in this proclamation until the story transforms all who hear it. To live for God's purposes is to proclaim his good news.

Take a few moments to share your assignments and reflections since the last meeting.

Dwelling in the Word

- Begin in prayer, inviting the Spirit to guide your group as you dwell in the text.
- Read aloud 2 Corinthians 5:11–6:1.
- Allow a few moments of silence after the reading has been completed to reflect on the passage and what stands out to you.
- Break into pairs (preferably with someone you don't know well) and discuss the following questions. Use this time to practice listening to each other as well as to the text.
    - What in the text captured your imagination?
    - What question would you most like to ask a biblical scholar?
- Gather once again as a large group and share your partners' responses.
- Review these responses and discuss: What might God be up to in the passage for us today?

Contextual Analysis

1. One of the midweek assignments from session 3 was to find an item in your context that reminded you of the bright and certain future God is bringing to his creation. If you haven't already, take time now to share the item you found and why it reminds you of God's good future.

2. Based on your experiences, what do people in your context think the Christian message about the future is? How do they understand it? What is their reaction to it?

3. What elements of the good news of God's salvation might be particularly important to the people in your context if they were to hear and believe it?

4. Look back over the contextual analysis done during previous sessions. Do the thoughts you recorded during those sessions add anything to your answers from today's analysis? If so, what?

Theological Reflection: *The God Who Brings Good News for All People*

The account of Jesus' birth in the Gospel of Luke tells of the angel saying to the shepherds, "Do not be afraid. I bring you good news that will cause great joy for all the people. Today in the town of David a Savior has been born to you; he is the Messiah, the Lord" (Lk 2:10-11). Jesus' coming was good news. In Luke 4:14-21 Jesus quotes the prophet Isaiah (see Is 61:1-2) and says that the Spirit of God has anointed him to proclaim good news. The good news Jesus was anointed to proclaim is a message about repairing what is broken, replacing despair with hope and inspiring righteousness where there was once only sin. Jesus preached this message wherever he went and trained his followers to do the same. He was good news and he proclaimed good news.

5. Read Luke 4:14-21. At this point, how would you define the good news of God proclaimed in and by Jesus?

6. Break into pairs and read some or all of the following passages. Take notes on how the good news of Jesus Christ is described: Luke 1:67-79; 1 Corinthians 15:20-28; Colossians 1:16-23; 2 Peter 3:8-13; Revelation 21:1-9.

7. Remain in your pairs. Based on all the texts you just read and the conversations you had during session 3, write a definition of the good news of God through Jesus Christ. Write the definition as you would on a Twitter account, using only 140 characters.

Missionary Imagination

JR Woodward asked fifty people to write a three–hundred– to five hundred–word article that summarized their understanding of the good news of the gospel. The fifty people were also asked to write the article in a way that would reflect their local context, as if they were writing an article to be published in their local newspaper. Woodward then compiled all fifty responses and published them in a brilliant little book titled *Viral Hope: Good News from the Urbs to the Burbs*.

8. As a group outline what you might include in an article summarizing the good news of God for your local context.

9. To whom, specifically, do you feel called to share this good news, and how could you proclaim it to them?

10. Pray as a group for the Spirit to empower you individually and communally to speak the good news to the people in your context.

Before We Meet Again

- Refine the three previous one-sentence descriptions you wrote in earlier weeks (if necessary). Add to them a fourth sentence that describes a life lived for the good news of God through Jesus Christ. Write all four sentences here.

- Turn your article outline into a full five hundred–word article. When your article is done, send it to the others in your group. Spend time this week reading each other's articles.

- Share your definition of the good news with those in your social network. Ask for feedback and record responses you get below. If you don't have Facebook or Twitter, consider sharing your definition through email or personal conversation.

- Consider also sharing your three to five hundred–word article with your social network. Again ask for feedback and record any responses you get in the following space.

Session Five

LIVING FOR THE BROKEN, THE SUFFERING AND THE MARGINALIZED

A man named George changed the way I think about living for God. George once asked me to help him find a place to stay because he was currently homeless. It was a busy week for me and our home was full, so even though George had become my friend over previous weeks, I told him the best I could do was set up a tent for him in the commons of the condominium where I live. George agreed, and we set him up with blankets, pillows and a nice tent. As I tried to sleep that night in my large, plush bed in my comfortably heated home, I couldn't help but think about Jesus' words in Matthew 25:40, "Truly I tell you, whatever you did for one of the least of these brothers and sisters of mine, you did for me." I had a hard time sleeping that night because I was haunted by this thought: *I just made Jesus sleep in my tent*. The next morning I determined to find ways to do more for the broken, the suffering and the marginalized. I decided living for God meant living for "the least of these brothers and sisters of mine."

Dwelling in the Word

- Begin in prayer, inviting the Spirit to guide your group as you dwell in the text.
- Read aloud 2 Corinthians 5:11–6:1.
- Allow a few moments of silence after the reading has been completed to reflect on the passage and what stands out to you.
- Break into pairs (preferably with someone you don't know well) and discuss the following questions. Use this time to practice listening to each other as well as to the text.
  - What in the text captured your imagination?
  - What question would you most like to ask a biblical scholar?
- Gather once again as a large group and share your partners' responses.
- Review these responses and discuss: What might God be up to in the passage for us today?

Contextual Analysis

Genesis describes creation as good and pleasing to God, and humans as made in his image and bringing him glory. When sin entered creation the beauty and goodness of creation experienced brokenness and imperfection. All of God's creation remains to this day both beautiful and broken, including the context in which you live. It is important that you recognize both.

Draw a stick figure with a smiley face on a large, poster-sized sheet of paper. Write the word *beautiful* somewhere on the page. Next draw a stick figure with a frowny face on a second large, poster-sized sheet of paper. Write the word *broken* somewhere on the page.

1. Spend 10-15 minutes as a group adding to each stick figure things that represent either the beauty of the local context or the brokenness. For instance, you might draw a big heart on the "beauty" drawing if you think your context is particularly loving. Or you might draw a wallet for the stick figure on the "broken" drawing if you feel your context is too greedy.

No context ever breaks down neatly into "beautiful" or "broken," but often we make generalizations that misappropriate those words. For example, we might assume that the suffering ones are broken while the elite, powerful or godly are beautiful. Stretch your thinking by answering the following questions about the subcategories of your context.

2. Who are the suffering and marginalized ones in your context? In what ways are they beautiful?

3. Who are the elite and powerful? What about them is broken? What is beautiful?

4. Who seems the most beautiful and godly? What about them is broken?

Theological Reflection: *The God Who Shows Compassion*

You've thought about your context, now think about God's heart for those in need.

5. Break into pairs and read Exodus 22:21-27 and Isaiah 41:17-20. What do these passages tell you about God?

6. Still in pairs, read some of the laws God gave his people in Leviticus 19:9-10; 25:35-36; Deuteronomy 14:28-29; 15:7-8; and 24:19-22. What do these laws have in common? What do these passages tell you about God and his purposes?

7. Using your previous knowledge of the Bible, list ways that Jesus showed compassion to those around him. Do the same for the followers of Jesus as depicted in Acts and in the rest of the New Testament.

8. Can you think of one text from the Bible that summarizes the passages we have read? If so, record it here. If not, write your own summary.

Missionary Imagination

The "least of these" in your context have been identified. The heart of God for "the least of these" has been explored. It's time to imagine what a life lived for the "least of these" might look like for you and your group.

9. Draw another stick figure on a large, poster-sized sheet of paper. Label this figure "A Missionary to ________________" (in the space write your context). Add drawings to the stick figure to represent what a missionary would look like if he or she were to live for the broken, the suffering and the marginalized in your local context.

Each person in the group should complete the following two sentences: (1) If I could snap my fingers and rid our local context of one broken thing, it would be ________________; (2) If I knew I could make a difference in someone's life and could not fail, I would ________________.

10. Spend time in prayer, asking for the Spirit of God to empower you to live for the broken, suffering and marginalized around you. When you have finished praying, discuss ways you feel your group can get involved in the lives of those in need. Choose at least one thing the group can do and write specific action steps here.

Before We Meet Again

- Review and refine all previous one-sentence descriptions you have written. Add a fifth sentence that describes a life lived for the broken, suffering and marginalized. Write the sentences in the following space.

- Take action! Look around you each day for ways to get involved in serving "the least of these." Bring very specific ideas to your next group gathering for how the group can get involved. Record your ideas here.

- Jesus instructs a rich man in Matthew 19:21 to sell his possessions and give to the poor. Most people who live in America are rich (an income of just $34,000 places someone in the top 1 percent globally of all income earners). Go through your possessions and sell as many of them as possible. Consider selling anything you haven't used in six months or a year. Also find at least one item of great value to you and sell it. Donate all proceeds to someone in need or to an organization that helps the marginalized. Consider making microfinance loans as well. For more information about microfinance loans, visit kiva.org or opportunity.org.

Session Six

LIVING IN SERVICE OF THE KINGDOM

The conversations in this guide have focused on what it might look like for your group to live on mission by considering how to live for God's purposes in your local contexts. One way to reflect on that mission is to ask, If ________________ [my context] were under God's reign, what would it look like?" Today's conversation will help you ask and answer that question by guiding you to think about the nature of God's kingdom, how it already exists around you, and what would change if it were fully established in your area.

Take a few moments to share about your assignments and reflections since the last meeting.

Dwelling in the Word

- Begin in prayer, inviting the Spirit to guide your group as you dwell in the text.

- Read aloud 2 Corinthians 5:11–6:1.
- Allow a few moments of silence after the reading has been completed to reflect on the passage and what stands out to you.
- Break into pairs (preferably with someone you don't know well) and discuss the following questions. Use this time to practice listening to each other as well as to the text.
    - What in the text captured your imagination?
    - What question would you most like to ask a biblical scholar?
- Gather once again as a large group and share your partners' responses.
- Review these responses and discuss: What might God be up to in the passage for us today?

Contextual Analysis

The kingdom of God is a major theme in the Bible, especially in the New Testament accounts of Jesus' preaching and in the writings of his followers. We can understand the kingdom of God as the place where God rules, where his creation joyfully recognizes and willingly submits to his authority.

1. To what extent is God's reign recognized and submitted to in your local context?

2. What alternative "kingdoms" are competing with God's kingdom for authority and power in your local context?

3. What in your context do you think *could* be brought under or included in the reign of God? What in your context is antithetical to the reign of God and either would need to be redeemed or destroyed if God were to reign fully?

Theological Reflection: *The God Who Reigns*

Scripture makes it clear that God reigns over all. If God reigns over all, then all of creation is his kingdom.

4. Psalms 95–99 are often labeled "Psalms of Enthronement" because of the way they focus on the fact that God reigns over his creation as King. Read and reflect together with the group upon Psalms 95 and 97. How do these short psalms describe God as King? How do they describe the reign of God? The kingdom of God?

Though God is King over all, parts of his creation live in rebellion. The kingdom of God exists on earth in the locations where God's purposes have already come to fruition, but elsewhere earth awaits the final culmination of God's kingdom. The parables of Jesus often described what it would be like when God's kingdom was realized (if only in part) on the earth.

5. Break into pairs. Each pair should select one of Jesus' parables about the kingdom, found in Matthew 13:1-52; 18:21-35; 20:1-16; 21:28-46; 22:1-14; 25:1-30. (Note: It is okay if not every text is selected.) For each parable, determine what can be learned about

the kingdom and what can be learned about the King. Report back to the group.

6. Jesus also taught his followers that being a part of his kingdom might not be what they expected. Consider some of Jesus' teaching about living for the kingdom in the following passages: Matthew 19:13-30; 25:31-46; Mark 10:17-31; Luke 9:57-62. What do these passages teach about the King and his kingdom?

Missionary Imagination

George Hunsberger, an American missiologist, defined the vocation of the church as the community, messenger and servant of the reign (or kingdom) of God.[7] Hunsberger also points to similar threefold descriptions others have developed to explain the mission or vocation of the church: being the witness, doing the witness, saying the witness; or speaking words of love, doing deeds of love, living a life of love; or mission of the truth (message), mission of the life (community), mission of the way (servant). Notice how each triad identifies something the church is, speaks and does as a representative of the kingdom of God.

7. Divide into three groups. In your smaller groups, imagine what it would look like for your whole group to be all three vocations: the community, messenger and servant of the kingdom of God.

8. Share your imagination with the larger group by writing a poem, drawing a picture and acting out a short skit, each for a different element of the church's vocation. Make sure you divide the tasks evenly so that each group does a creative project for each of the elements, and so that each element is depicted in all three ways.

Final Assignments

- Review and refine the five one-sentence descriptions you have written. Add to them a sixth sentence describing a life lived in service of God's kingdom. Write all six sentences here.

- Use your six sentences to come up with one or two creative projects that summarize or represent the learning you experienced throughout the six conversations your group had. You could write a limerick, make a collage, write a play, pen lyrics to a song, shoot a video or something similar. It's up to you! Be creative and have fun.
- Schedule a time for your group to get together to share a meal, go over each other's six sentences and see your creative projects. Have fun! Make it a celebration and don't forget to applaud everyone's learning and creativity!
- Continue to read and reflect on passages from the Bible that describe the reign and rule of God in his kingdom:
    1. The enthronement psalms: Psalms 95–99

2. Jesus' parables on the kingdom: Matthew 13:1-52; 18:21-35; 20:1-16; 21:28-46; 22:1-14; 25:1-30
3. Jesus' teaching about living for the kingdom: Matthew 19:13-30; 25:31-46; Mark 10:17-31; Luke 9:57-62

- One of the elements of the prayer Jesus taught his disciples to pray is

  "Our Father in heaven,
  hallowed be your name,
  your kingdom come,
  your will be done,
  on earth as it is in heaven." (Mt 6:9-10)

  Spend time in prayer every day this week, recognizing God as the holy king and asking for him to bring his kingdom to earth as it is in heaven (the realm where God's rule is complete). Record some of your prayers in the following space.

- It is often said that teaching is the best form of learning. Therefore, identify 2-6 other people in your life who you could take through the material covered during your study or the key learning you gleaned from the conversations. Use this conversation guide or create your own process to take your friends through a learning journey with you.

Appendix

TIPS FOR HAVING GREAT SMALL GROUP GATHERINGS

The following tips were gleaned from my experience in small group ministry. Practice these over the course of your time together, but know they are not exhaustive. Space has been left at the end for your group to add its own tips for having great small group gatherings.

TIP 1: *Be Prepared*

Group gatherings flourish when folks come prepared. If there is one person designated to lead or facilitate the gathering, that person should be in prayer throughout the week, asking God's Spirit to lead him or her and to be present at the gathering. The leader or facilitator should also personally work through the material a couple of times so he or she can create a gathering that flows smoothly and achieves the desired objectives.

It is also important for group members to come prepared. Their preparation includes completing midweek assignments, bringing required materials, opening their minds to what God might want to say and opening their lives to where the Spirit might want to lead.

TIP 2: *Foster Habits That Create Good Conversation and Discussion*

There is a reason these guides have been titled Forge Guides for Missional Conversation. They are meant to *create conversation* about living missionally! It is important that groups foster habits that help create good conversation. These habits include:

- Directing discussion toward all group members, not just the facilitator. Often when someone responds to a question, he or she will look at the person who asked the question. Group members should look at and interact with one another while giving their responses, not just the leader.
- Avoid the silent head nod, which is one of the biggest conversation killers. Unfortunately, it is a hard habit to break. However, when someone shares or offers a response, the group should work to give more of a response than the silent nod. Perhaps someone could ask a question, share their own insight, request for the person to say more or even just say thanks.
- Ask good questions and follow-up questions. The questions provided for you in the conversation guides will hopefully be effective at sparking conversations. It is imperative that the group does not merely answer the questions provided but asks new questions as the conversation continues. Asking new questions is a good indication that group members are listening to one another and taking an active interest in what is being said.
- Draw answers out of each participant. One of the cardinal sins of teaching or leading a discussion is to answer your own question to avoid the awkward silence. If a question is asked and no one answers after you have allowed for a comfortable time of silence, con-

sider repeating or rephrasing the question. Also consider calling on a specific person to answer. Most of the time the person called on will have something insightful to share. I often am amazed at what the quietest people in groups have to say when a leader calls on them to specifically share. As a last resort, suggest that the group come back to the question later, or give time for individuals to share with their neighbor before sharing with everyone.

- As much as possible, affirm what others say. People feel affirmed when their thoughts are repeated or referred to later in the discussion. When people feel affirmed, they are more likely to continue to participate in the conversation.
- Clarify or summarize what has been said. Sometimes a group member will offer a long answer or get sidetracked onto a different discussion. It is often helpful for the group leader or another member to summarize what has been said, even asking for clarity if necessary. This clarifying practice will help keep the conversation moving in a focused direction.

TIP 3: *Share Leadership and Always Give People Something to Contribute*

Small groups flourish when all members are given a chance to lead on a regular basis and when all members are expected to contribute to each gathering. Rotate leadership and facilitating responsibilities while working through this guide if at all possible. Always try to find ways to ensure everyone is bringing something to contribute, whether an activity to plan or simply a snack to share.

TIP 4: *Encourage and Affirm One Another as Much as Possible*

A little bit of affirmation goes such a long way in small groups. Telling someone he or she had a good idea, did a good job leading, brought good energy to the group or made a nice snack will encourage the person to continue to participate in group gatherings in important ways. Groups that are able to identify each other's strengths and to encourage those strengths to be used more will be full of life, energy and possibility.

TIP 5: *Create Space for Feedback*

Group gatherings will be better over the long run if the group can create a regular rhythm of giving and receiving feedback about group gatherings. Allowing all members to give input or offer ideas for future gatherings will increase ownership and help craft an experience unique to the group.

RECOMMENDED RESOURCES FOR FURTHER STUDY

I have had the privilege to teach on all things related to the missional church in a wide variety of settings. It is a common occurrence for me to discover that those who joined me in the learning experience often are only aware of one small portion of the missional church movement. Most folks I meet seem to only have one or two authors or teachers who have encouraged them to think and live more missionally. Consequently, these folks often have only one or two ideas of what it might look like for a Christian or a church to think and live missionally. I always love watching their expressions of surprise and joy when I tell them that the missional church conversation has been going on for over a century and has produced hundreds of books and dozens of different ideas for what the missional church might actually look like in reality. More than anything, though, I love to watch their imaginations grow as they encounter fresh voices and new ideas.

If you would like to broaden your missional imagination even further than you have already done through this study guide, the following resources will help you.

1. "A Brief History of the Missional Church Movement." This short essay describes the growth of the missional church movement from the World Missionary Conference in Edinburgh (1910) through today, identifying a variety of sources that have funded the movement. You can find this essay online at www.ivpress.com.

2. "Helpful Resources for Developing Missional Imagination." This list of resources is given to everyone who plays a leadership role in the Forge Mission Training Network so that they can expand their own imaginations for mission and help others do the same. You can view the list at www.ivpress.com. For more information on the books, you can view my list at www.worldcat.org/profiles/luthercml3/lists/2934221.

Notes

[1]Alan Hirsch, "Defining Missional," *Leadership Journal*, fall 2008, www.christianitytoday.com/le/2008/fall/17.20.html.

[2]"Dwelling in the Word" is a practice developed and taught to me by Dr. Patrick Keifert of Church Innovations (www.churchinnovations.org). The instructions provided are a slightly modified version of the guide provided in Patrick Keifert and Pat Taylor Ellison, *Dwelling in the Word: A Pocket Handbook* (Minneapolis: Church Innovations Institute, 2011). For more on Dwelling in the Word, visit www.churchinnovations.org/06_about/dwelling.html.

[3]David H. Kelsey, *To Understand God Truly: What's Theological About a Theological School?* (Louisville: Westminster/John Knox Press, 1992).

[4]David J. Bosch, *Transforming Mission: Paradigm Shifts in Theology of Mission* (Maryknoll, NY: Orbis, 1991).

[5]Ibid., p. 10.

[6]Jürgen Moltmann, *Theology of Hope: On the Ground and the Implications of a Christian Eschatology*, trans. James W. Leitch, 5th ed. (London: SCM Press, 2002), p. 17.

[7]George Hunsberger, "Missional Vocation: Called and Sent to Represent the Reign of God," in *Missional Church: A Vision for the Sending of the Church in North America*, ed. Darrell L. Guder (Grand Rapids: Eerdmans, 1998).

Forge Guides
for Missional Conversation

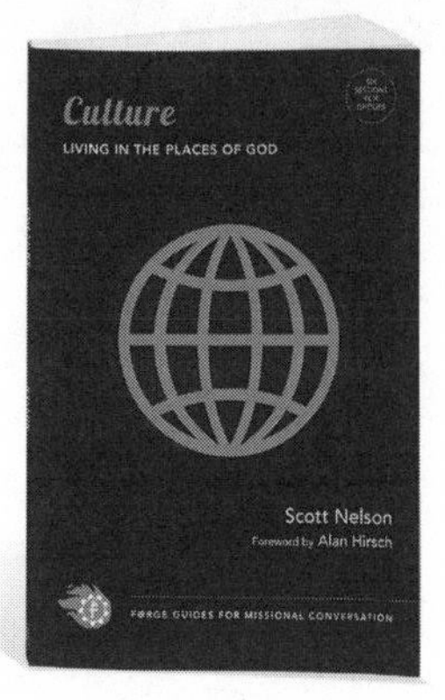

COMMUNITY: *Living as the People of God*
MISSION: *Living for the Purposes of God*
POWER: *Living by the Spirit of God*
VISION: *Living Under the Promises of God*
CULTURE: *Living in the Places of God*

How can God's people give witness to his kingdom in an increasingly post-Christian culture? How can the church recover its true mission in the face of a world in need? Forge America exists to help birth and nurture the missional church in America and beyond. Books published by InterVarsity Press that bear the Forge imprint will also serve that purpose.

Forge Books from InterVarsity Press

Creating a Missional Culture, JR Woodward

Forge Guides for Missional Conversation (set of five), Scott Nelson

The Missional Quest, Lance Ford and Brad Brisco

More Than Enchanting, Jo Saxton

The Story of God, the Story of Us, Sean Gladding

For more information on Forge America, to apply for a Forge residency, or to find or start a Forge hub in your area, visit **www.forgeamerica.com**

For more information about Forge books from InterVarsity Press, including forthcoming releases, visit **www.ivpress.com/forge**